Quick How to Read Music

Simple Search

No-Fuss, Flick-thru Guides

Jake Jackson

Publisher and Creative Director: Nick Wells

Project, design and media integration: Jake Jackson

Website and software: David Neville with Stevens Dumpala and Steve Moulton

Editorial: Gillian Whitaker

First published 2022 by
FLAME TREE PUBLISHING
6 Melbray Mews
Fulham, London SW6 3NS
United Kingdom
flametreepublishing.com

Music information site:
flametreemusic.com

26 25 24 23 22
10 9 8 7 6 5 4 3 2 1

© 2022 Flame Tree Publishing Ltd

Images and text © 2022 Jake Jackson

ISBN: 978-1-83964-947-9

Printed and bound in the UK by Clays Ltd Elcograf S.p.A.

The CIP record for this book is available from the British Library.

Jake Jackson is a writer and musician. He has created and contributed to over 20 practical music books, including *Reading Music Made Easy*, *Play Flamenco* and *Piano and Keyboard Chords*. His music is available on iTunes, Amazon and Spotify amongst others.

See & Hear
Web Links

Instrument
& Voice

Quick How to Read Music

Simple
Search

No-Fuss,
Flick-thru
Guides

Jake Jackson

Flame Tree
Music
CHORDS • SCALES
flametreemusic.com

Contents

 Online access
flametreemusic.com Scan the code to
hear chords & scales

4

10 SIMPLE STEPS

Online access
flametreemusic.com

**Scan the code to
hear chords & scales**

How to Use This Book

This book is divided into 10 sections which lead you through the basics of reading music. Each spread is direct and simple, designed to help with the constant reminders and repetition necessary for learning music. **QUICK HOW TO READ MUSIC** will also be a useful companion for later use when you need an easy and accessible reference to musical terms.

The steps are:

1. **The Basics.** This step introduces you to the basic concepts: the stave (or staff), lines, spaces, ledger lines, clefs and middle C.

2. **Treble Clef.** This section covers notes above middle C and helps you remember names for notes on lines and spaces.

3. **The Bass Clef.** This section covers notes below middle C and offers different ways of remembering notes on lines and spaces.

4. **Notes.** This step shows how long to sound each type of note as you begin to understand about the pulse and time of music.

5. **Rests.** For every note there is a corresponding rest, because where no notes are played a rest will be inserted.

6. **Time Signatures.** A time signature tells us how many notes and rests will appear in each bar of music, and determines the pulse of the music.

7. **Sharps, Flats & Naturals.** These alter the pitch of a note, with sharps and flats often played on the black notes of a piano.

8. **Key Signatures.** This step shows you how to identify the key of a piece of music, using flats and sharp signs.

9. **Scales.** Four scales for each key are provided in ascending and descending patterns, in notation and guitar tab forms.

10. **Chords from Scales.** Chords can be used to accompany melodies. This step shows you how to identify and construct chords for each major key.

Other information is also provided:

Symbols & Marks. A simple reference to the primary marks of expression and dynamic used in music pieces.

Going Online. flametreemusic.com offers the next steps for a wider understanding of music, offering sound links, scales, chords and other resources.

Online access
flametreemusic.com

Scan the code to
hear chords & scales

About the Website

The Flame Tree Music website allows you to hear and search chords and scales. It complements our range of books and offers easy access to chords online and on the move, through tablets, smartphones, desktop computers and books.

- The website offers access to chord diagrams and finger positions for both the guitar and the piano/keyboard, presenting a wide range of **audio** options to help develop good listening technique, and to assist you in identifying the chord and each note within it.

- The site offers **12 free chords per key,** those most commonly used in bands and songwriting.

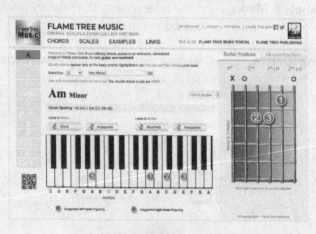

Online access
flametreemusic.com

**Scan the code to
hear chords & scales**

HOW TO READ MUSIC

- A subscription is available if you'd like the full range of chords, 50 for each key.

- Guitar chords are shown with first and second positions on the fretboard. Options are also given for Left-hand players.

- For the keyboard, you can see and hear each note in left- and right-hand positions.

- Choose the key, then the chord name from the drop down menu. Note that the red chords are available free. Those in blue can be accessed with a subscription.

- Once you've selected the chord, press **GO** and the details of the chord will be shown, with chord spellings, keyboard and guitar fingerings. Sounds are provided in four different configurations.

- flametreemusic.com also gives you access to **20 scales for each key.**

Online access
flametreemusic.com

Scan the code to
hear chords & scales

The Audio Links

Requirements: a camera and internet-ready smartphone (e.g. iPhone, any Android phone (e.g. Samsung Galaxy), Nokia Lumia, or camera-enabled tablet such as the iPad Mini). The best result is achieved using a Wi-Fi connection.

Either:

1. Point your camera at the QR code. Most modern smartphones read the link automatically and offer you the website **flametreemusic.com** to connect online.

Or:

1. Download any **free QR code reader**. An app store search will reveal a great many of these, so obviously it's best to go with the ones with the highest ratings and don't be afraid to try a few before you settle on the one that works best for you. Tapmedia's QR Code Reader app, Kaspersky QR Scanner or QR Code Reader by Scan are perfectly fine, although some of the free apps also have ads.

2. On your smartphone, open the app and **scan** the **QR code** at the base of any particular page.

Online access
flametreemusic.com

Scan the code to
hear chords & scales

Then:

3. Scanning any code will bring you to the home page. From there you can access and **hear** the complete library of scales and chords on **flametreemusic.com**.

    On pages where QR codes feature alongside particular chords and scales, those codes will take you directly to the relevant chord or scale on the website.

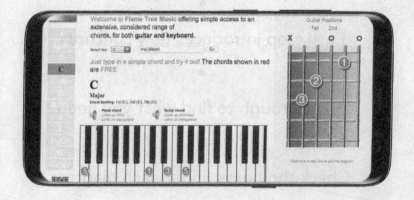

4. Use the drop-down menu to choose from **20 scales** or 12 **free chords** (50 with subscription) per key.

5. Click the sounds! Both piano and guitar audio is provided. This is particularly helpful when you're playing with others.

    The QR codes give you direct access to chords and scales. You can access a much wider range of chords if you register.

 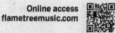

Easy Access

Organized in 10 steps

•

Each step introduces new concepts

•

Flick through to find what you need

•

Check the notes under each diagram

•

The QR codes allow you to hear

the scales and chords

•

Online access
flametreemusic.com Scan the code to
hear chords & scales

Quick How to Read Music

Simple Search

No-Fuss, Flick-thru Guides

FLAMETREEMUSIC.COM
ONLINE LINKS

Online access
flametreemusic.com

Scan the code to
hear chords & scales

Quick How to Read Music

Simple Search

1

STEP 1

THE BASICS

Music is created by people singing and
playing a wide variety of instruments.
Writing down and reading the music is
an important part of music-making.

The following pages will introduce you to
the very basic concepts: what is a stave?
What are lines and spaces? What are
ledger lines and clefs?

This section closes with the note called
middle C, the understanding of which
will give you a solid foundation for
the rest of the book.

Online access
flametreemusic.com   Scan the code to
hear chords & scales

15

Stave or Staff

These five lines make up the stave (sometimes called staff).

The stave is the backbone to the body of the music, it holds the **notes** and the

rests and the various **symbols** that tell you how to play loudly or softly, when

to repeat and when to stop.

The stave allows us to indicate **pitch**, whether a sound is high or low.

The highest sounds
appear at the top of
a stave.

The lowest sounds
appear at the bottom
of a stave.

Lines

The stave is always made up of five lines. Notes can be written on the lines or the spaces.

Each line on a stave represents a particular musical note, although which note depends on which **clef** is shown at the beginning of the music (clefs are covered on pages 26–31).

It is worth noting that the lines also show the music **moving** in time from **start** to **finish**, and should always be read from **left** to **right**.

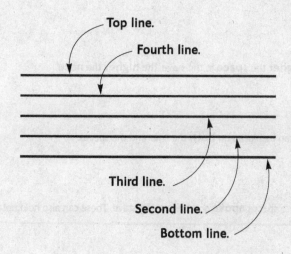

Top line.

Fourth line.

Third line.

Second line.

Bottom line.

Spaces

Between the five lines there are four spaces. Notes can be

placed in these spaces.

The **higher** the **space** in the stave, the **higher** the **note**.

Notes can be placed on **both** the lines and the spaces.

There are spaces **above** and **below** the stave. These can also hold notes.

Online access
flametreemusic.com Scan the code to
hear chords & scales

20

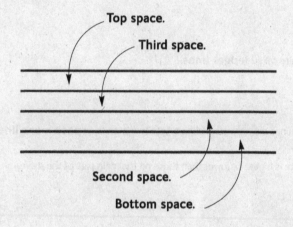

Top space.

Third space.

Second space.

Bottom space.

Ledger Lines

Often you will see music with small lines written above or below the main part of the stave.

These are called **ledger lines**.

Ledger lines are only used when a note is written in a **space** or on a **line** where the note is higher or lower than those on the main part of the stave.

Ledger lines are written at equal distances from the main lines.

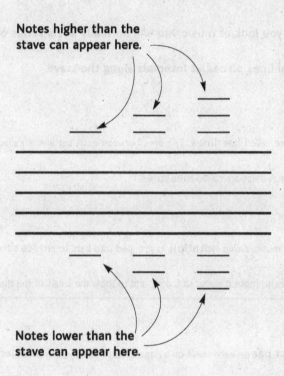

Notes higher than the stave can appear here.

Notes lower than the stave can appear here.

The Bars

When you look at music you will normally see a series of vertical lines placed at intervals along the stave.

These are called **bar lines**. The area between each bar line is called a **bar**. Sometimes these are called **measures**.

Written music, called **notation**, is grouped into bars to provide structure to the notes, to make it easier to follow, and to show the **beat** of the music.

The **first bar** on each stave on a page of music always carries a **clef** symbol in place of the first bar line.

These are bars.

These are bar lines.

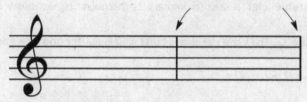

This is a treble clef.

Introducing the Treble Clef

A clef symbol is written at the beginning of a piece of music, and at the beginning, on the left side, of every stave.

The **treble clef** is used for instruments that sound higher, usually above **middle C**. The treble clef always **curls** around the **second line** from the bottom of the stave.

Instruments that commonly use the treble clef are the violin, guitar, treble recorder, saxophone, trumpet and the right hand on a piano.

Children's and female **voices** use the treble clef.

Online access
flametreemusic.com Scan the code to
hear chords & scales

26

The curl of the treble clef wraps around the second line up from the bottom line.

5

4

3

2

1

Numbered from the bottom line upwards.

Introducing the Bass Clef

The bass clef is used for instruments and voices which sound

lower, especially those that provide the bass sounds in a piece.

The bass clef is always written so that the two dots sit either side of the fourth

line up from the bottom of the stave.

Instruments that commonly use the bass clef are the cello, bassoon, tuba,

bass guitar and the left hand on a piano or any other keyboard instrument, such

as an organ.

Male baritone, tenor and bass **voices** use the bass clef.

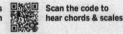

The two dots of the bass clef sit either side of fourth line up from the bottom line.

5
4
3
2
1

Numbered from the bottom line upwards.

The C Clef

Other clefs are occasionally used for different instruments to make the reading of them easier. These include the alto clef and the tenor clef (also called C clefs).

The **alto clef** can be used by the viola. The middle of this clef sits on the line that normally holds the middle C.

The **tenor clef** can be used by the cello, bassoon and trombone. It also sits on the line of the middle C but the five bar lines shift down to provide a space and line below the bottom edge of the clef.

The middle of the alto clef
sits on the line that normally
shows middle C.

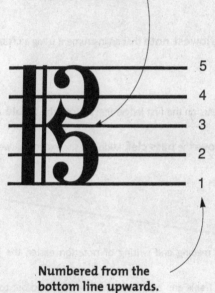

5
4
3
2
1

Numbered from the
bottom line upwards.

Middle C

The note called middle C appears in the middle of the piano.

It is usually the **lowest note** that an instrument using a **treble clef** can play.

Middle C appears on the first ledger line **below** the **treble clef** and the first ledger line **above** the **bass clef**. Middle C sits exactly between the treble and bass clef staves.

To make the reading and writing of notation easier, the gap between the staves of the treble and bass clef is usually stretched out to allow a middle C on **both** staves.

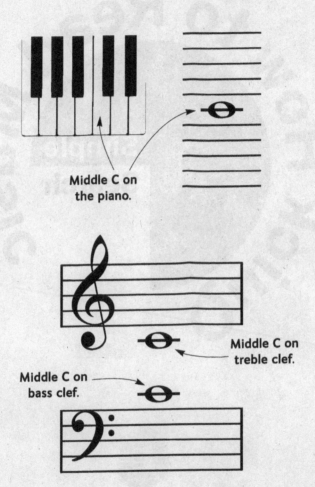

Middle C on the piano.

Middle C on treble clef.

Middle C on bass clef.

Online access
flametreemusic.com

Scan the code to
hear chords & scales

Quick How to Read Music

Simple Search

2

STEP 2

TREBLE CLEF

The treble clef is used for notes above middle C.
On the piano this applies generally to the music
played with the right hand.

Instruments such as the trumpet, violin and the
clarinet also use the treble clef, along with higher
voices such as the soprano (or treble) sounds of
children and female singers.

This chapter offers more detailed information
on the treble clef and provides ways to remember
the notes of the lines and spaces.

Treble Clef Line Notes

A good way to remember the names for those notes that appear on the lines of the treble clef is to use a mnemonic to remind you:

Food

Deserves

Boy

Good

Every

Read from the bottom up.

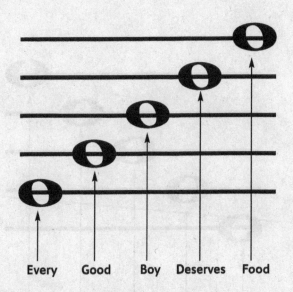

Every   Good   Boy   Deserves   Food

Treble Clef Line Notes on Keyboard

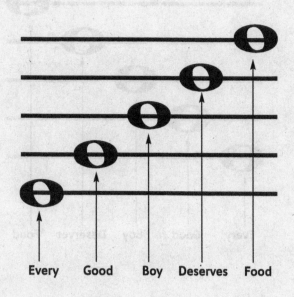

Every   Good   Boy   Deserves   Food

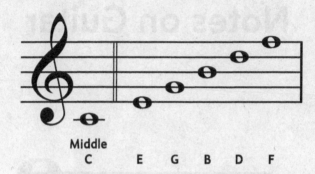

Middle
C   E   G   B   D   F

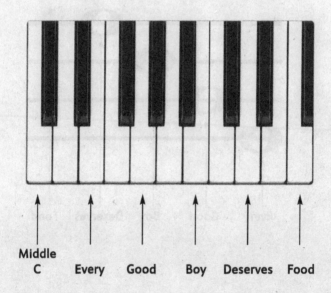

Middle
C   Every   Good   Boy   Deserves   Food

Treble Clef Line Notes on Guitar

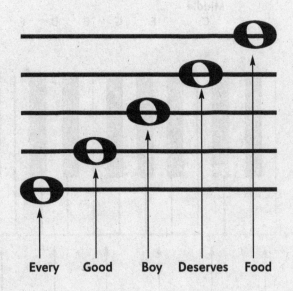

Every   Good   Boy   Deserves   Food

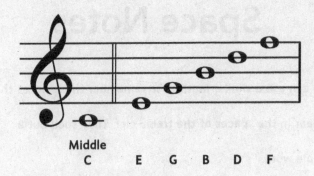

Middle
C   E   G   B   D   F

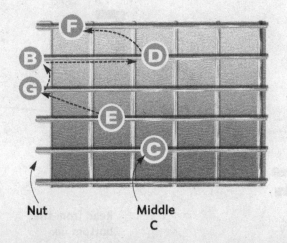

Nut   Middle
C

The diagram here is from the player's view. Treble clef line notes on a guitar are spread across the strings. The notes G and B are shown here on the open strings.

Treble Clef
Space Notes

You can use a similar method to remember those notes that

appear in the spaces of the treble clef. They spell out a

simple word:

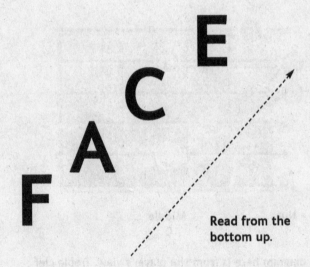

E

C

A

F

Read from the
bottom up.

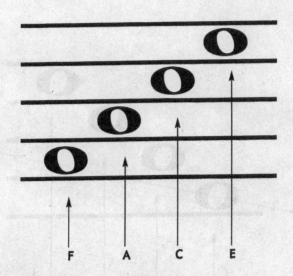

F   A   C   E

Treble Clef Space Notes on Keyboard

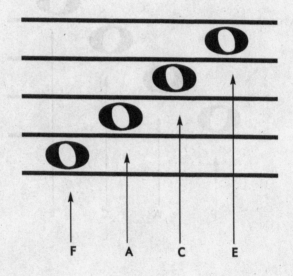

F   A   C   E

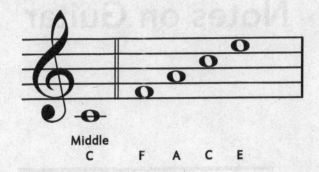

Middle
C   F   A   C   E

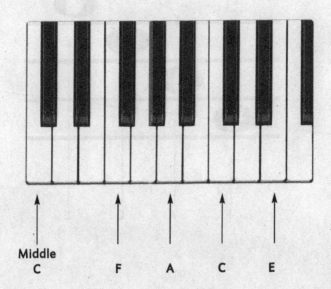

Middle
C   F   A   C   E

Treble Clef Space Notes on Guitar

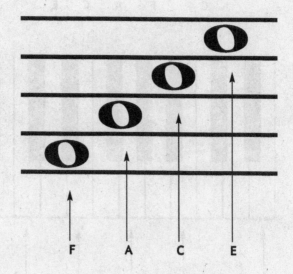

F   A   C   E

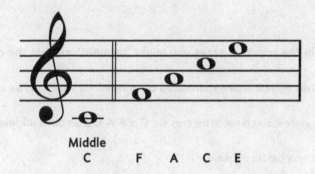

Middle
C   F   A   C   E

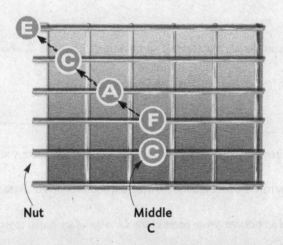

Nut   Middle
C

Again, the diagram here is from the player's view with
the treble clef open notes played across the strings.
The top note E is shown here on the open string.

Octaves

From the previous pages you might have noticed that the note names appear more than once on a stave. For instance, in the treble clef, in the spaces between the lines, the **C** of **F A C E** is **above middle C**, which sits **below** the stave.

This occurs because, in standard western music, there are **7** whole **note names**, from **A** to **G**, which are then repeated.

If you listen to the sound of middle C and the sound of the C above, you will hear that they have the same quality. The **interval** between notes of the same name is called an **octave**. When notes of the same name are played together they create a rich, enhanced sound.

Online access
flametreemusic.com   Scan the code to
hear chords & scales

48

The interval between the two C notes is an octave.

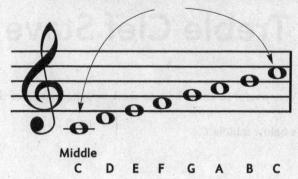

Middle
C D E F G A B C

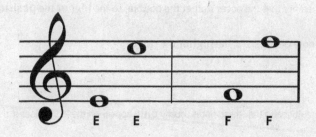

E E F F

Examples of other octaves.

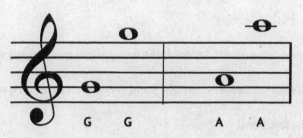

G G A A

Notes Below the Treble Clef Stave

It is very useful to know how to work out the names of the notes below middle C.

Remember that the notes start at the bottom, so the **higher** the **position** of the note on the stave, the **higher** the **note**.

Remember also that these notes usually **only** appear on the ledger lines **if** there is **no bass clef**.

However, in piano music, **ledger lines** are sometimes used to signify that the notes should be played by the **right hand**, with the **bass clef** being reserved for the **left hand**.

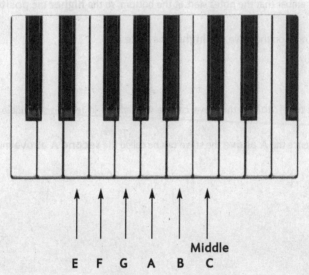

Notes Above the Treble Clef Stave

It is also useful to know how to work out the names of the notes above the stave.

Remember that the notes start at the bottom, so the **higher** the **position** of the note on the stave, the **higher** the **note**.

The notes **above** the stave can be worked out in relation to middle C. For instance the **A above** the stave can be called the **second A above** middle C.

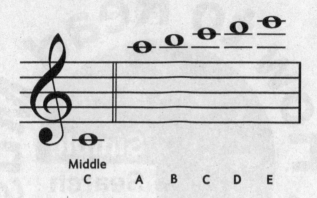

Middle
C   A   B   C   D   E

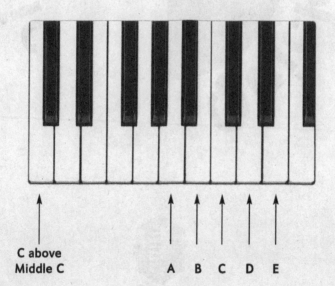

C above
Middle C   A   B   C   D   E

Online access
flametreemusic.com

Scan the code to
hear chords & scales

53

Quick How to Read Music

Simple Search

3

STEP 3

BASS CLEF

The bass clef is used for notes below middle C. On the piano this applies generally to the music played with the left hand.

Instruments such as the trombone, tuba and the bass guitar also use the bass clef, along with lower voices such as the tenor and bass sounds of adult male singers.

This chapter offers more detailed information on the bass clef and provides ways to remember the notes on the lines and spaces.

Online access
flametreemusic.com

Scan the code to
hear chords & scales

Bass Clef
Line Notes

As with the treble clef, a good way to remember the names

for those notes that appear on the lines of the bass clef is to

use a mnemonic to remind you:

Anything
Forget
Don't
Boys
Good

Read from the
bottom up.

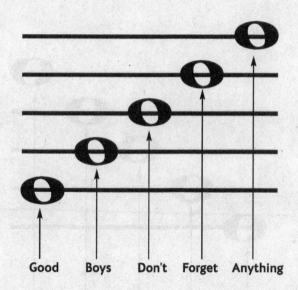

Good   Boys   Don't   Forget   Anything

Bass Clef Line Notes on Keyboard

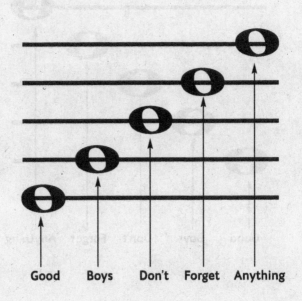

| Good | Boys | Don't | Forget | Anything |

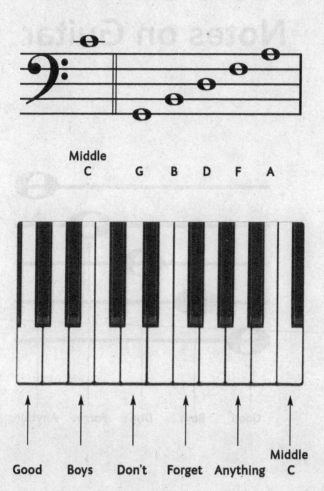

Bass Clef Line Notes on Guitar

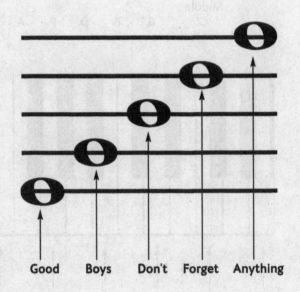

Good   Boys   Don't   Forget   Anything

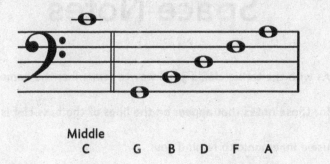

Middle
C   G   B   D   F   A

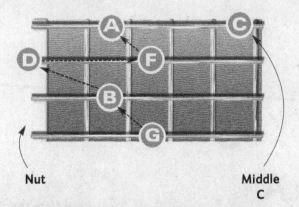

Nut   Middle
C

The diagram here is from the player's view. Bass clef
line notes on a bass guitar are spread across the
strings. The note D is shown on the open string.

Online access
flametreemusic.com   Scan the code to
hear chords & scales

61

Bass Clef Space Notes

As with the treble clef, a good way to remember the names for those notes that appear on the lines of the bass clef is to use a mnemonic to remind you:

Grass

Eat

Cows

All

Read from the bottom up.

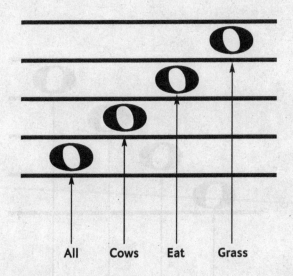

All   Cows   Eat   Grass

Bass Clef Space Notes on Keyboard

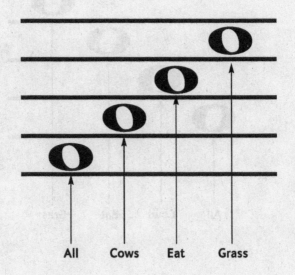

All   Cows   Eat   Grass

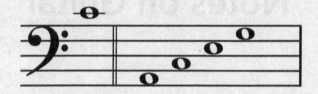

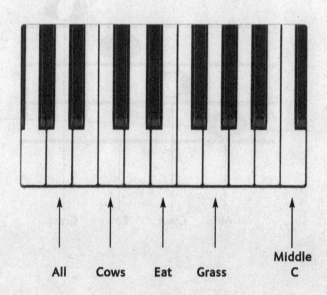

Bass Clef Space Notes on Guitar

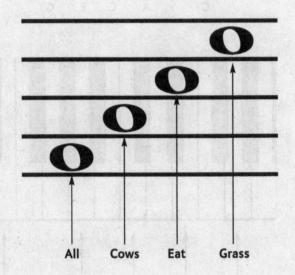

All   Cows   Eat   Grass

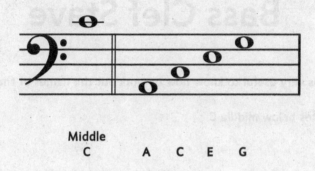

Middle
C   A   C   E   G

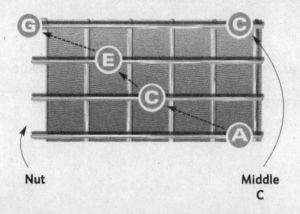

Nut   Middle
C

The diagram here is from the player's view. Bass clef
line notes on a bass guitar are spread across the
strings. The note G is shown on the open string.

Notes Below the Bass Clef Stave

It is very useful to know how to work out the names of the notes below middle C.

Remember that the notes start at the bottom, so the **lower** the **position** of the note on the stave, the **lower** the **note**.

As a guide, a cello would normally only make notes as low as the C two octaves below middle C.

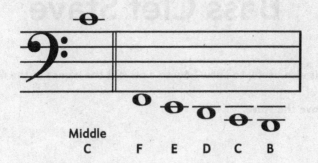

Middle
C   F   E   D   C   B

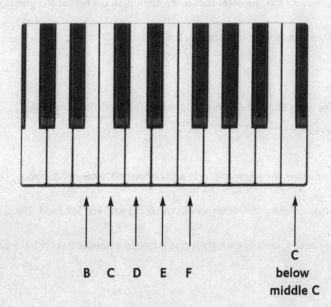

B   C   D   E   F   C
below
middle C

Notes Above the Bass Clef Stave

It is also useful to know how to work out the names of the notes above the stave.

Remember that the notes start at the bottom, so the **higher** the **position** of the note on the stave, the **higher** the note.

The notes **above** the stave can be worked out in relation to **middle C**.

Remember, the ledger lines only apply wherre no treble clef is used, or, on the piano, to show that notes should be played with the left hand. The **G** note opposite is normally the highest note played by a **double bass** or **bass guitar**.

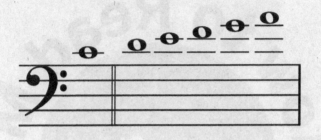

Middle
C   D   E   F   G   A

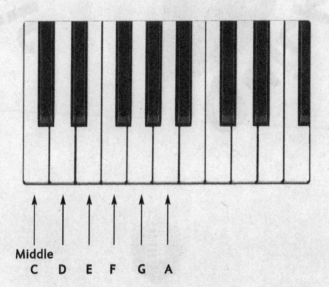

Middle
C   D   E   F   G   A

Quick How to Read Music

Simple Search

4

LEARN TO PLAY · CHORDS SCALES
FLAMETREEMUSIC.COM
ONLINE LINKS

STEP 4

NOTES

Notes are the main building blocks of
every musical piece.

The position of the note on a particular stave
tells you which note to play.

The look of the note tells you how long to sound
the note and therefore gives you clues about
the pulse of the music and how it relates to the
time signature (*see* page 107).

Notes can be grouped together and must be
replaced by an equivalent rest (*see* page 95) if no
sound is to be played.

Parts of a Note

Notes are made up of four main parts:

1. The **notehead** is either hollow or filled.

2. The **tail** occurs on notes with shorter lengths – quavers and shorter notes.

3. A **beam** is used when connecting notes of the same value. The shorter the

   length of the note, the greater the number of beams. A semiquaver has two

   tails, so it has two beams when connected to other semiquavers.

4. A **dot** is used to add half the length of the note. A quaver without a dot is

   worth two semiquavers. With a dot this increases to three.

Tail

Stem →

Notehead

Dot

Beam

This is a rest (*see* page 95)

Whole Note/ Semibreve

A semibreve is a note that fills the whole bar, hence the alternative name: whole note.

A semibreve has a **hollow notehead**, with no stem, tail, beams or dots.

A semibreve is equal to two minims, four crotchets or eight quavers.

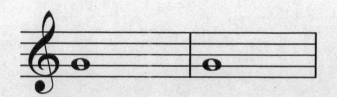

Half Note/ Minim

A minim is a note that fills half of a whole bar, hence the

alternative name: half note.

A minim has a **hollow notehead** and a stem, but no tail or beams. It can

be dotted.

A semibreve is equal to two crotchets, four quavers or eight semiquavers.

Quarter Note/ Crotchet

A crotchet is a note that makes up a quarter of the whole bar, hence the alternative name: quarter note.

A crotchet has a **filled-in notehead** and a stem, but no tail or beams. It can be dotted.

A crotchet is equal to half a minim, two quavers or four semiquavers.

Eighth Note/ Quaver

A quaver is a note that makes up an eighth of the whole bar,

hence the alternative name: eighth note.

A quaver has a filled-in notehead, a stem, **a tail** and beams. It can be dotted.

A quaver is equal to two semiquavers.

A single quaver is written with its tail, but quavers are more commonly found in

groups with a bar across, to make them easier to read.

This is a quaver rest.

Sixteenth Note/ Semiquaver

A semiquaver is a note that makes up a sixteenth of the whole bar, hence the alternative name: sixteenth note.

A semiquaver has a filled-in notehead, a stem and two tails or double beams. It can be dotted. A semiquaver is equal to two demisemiquavers.

A semiquaver is written with its tails, but they are often found in groups with a beam across, to make them easier to read. The presence of semiquavers usually indicates a fast passage of music.

There are further, shorter notes, with more tails.

Dotted Notes

The length of the sound of a note can be increased by one half, by adding a single dot to the right-hand side of the notehead.

A **dotted minim** has the same musical length as three crotchets, instead of the usual two, so leaving space for a single crotchet or crotchet rest in the example opposite.

A **dotted crotchet** has the same music length as three quavers.

A **dotted quaver** has the same value as three semiquavers.

Triplets

Triplets are indicated with a **3** above a group of three notes.

Triplets are three identical notes tied together to fill the space of **two** equivalent notes.

Three **crotchets** grouped as a triplet have the same time value as two crotchets, but **sound faster** because the three notes are played.

Three **quavers** grouped as a triplet have the same time value as two quavers, but sound faster because the three quavers are played.

**The triplet of quavers above has the same
time value as two quavers below.**

Online access
flametreemusic.com **Scan the code to
hear chords & scales**

89

Ties

Ties are curved lines that connect two notes of the same pitch. The line is drawn from notehead to notehead.

Ties are used within a bar to connect two notes where their total value does not have a unique symbol or note. For instance, this is useful for creating the length of a crotchet and a quaver, or a dotted crotchet and a crotchet together.

Ties allow a note to be extended **across** a **bar line**.

Online access
flametreemusic.com

Scan the code to
hear chords & scales

90

Ties within a bar.

Tie across a bar line.

Slurs

Slurs look like ties but they are not the same.

A slur indicates that the music within the start and end points should be played **smoothly**.

A slur can connect notes of **different** pitches.

A slur can **stretch across** several **bars**.

Quick How to Read Music

Simple Search

5

STEP 5

RESTS

For every note there is a corresponding rest.

When looking at a bar of music it is
important to realize that each bar must add
up to the number of beats set out at the
beginning of the piece. Where no notes are
to be played, a rest is put in their place to
even out the beats.

The look of the rest tells you
how long to wait.

Whole Note/ Semibreve Rest

The semibreve rest sits under the fourth line from the bottom line of the stave.

The semibreve rest has the same length as a **semibreve** note.

The standard musical bar contains four beats. A semibreve rest lasts for a **whole bar** of four beats.

If a bar only has three beats, the semibreve rest fills the whole bar too.

Note   Rest

Half Note/
Minim Rest

The minim rest sits on top of the third line from the bottom

line of the stave.

The minim rest has the same length as a half note, or **minim**, note.

The standard musical bar contains four beats.

A minim rest lasts for a **half** a **bar** and so is equal to two beats.

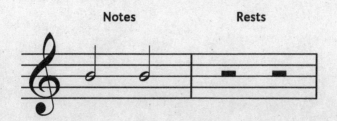

Notes   Rests

Quarter Note/ Crotchet Rest

The crotchet rest is half the length of the minim rest. It has the same length as a quarter note, or crotchet.

The standard musical bar contains four beats.

A crotchet rest lasts for a **quarter** of a **bar** and so is equal to one beat.

Notes   **Rests**

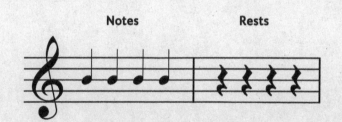

Eighth Note/ Quaver Rest

The quaver rest is half the length of the crotchet rest. It has the same length as an eighth note, or quaver.

The standard musical bar contains four beats.

A quaver rest lasts for an **eighth** of a **bar** and so is equal to half a beat.

Online access
flametreemusic.com Scan the code to
hear chords & scales

102

Notes   **Rests**

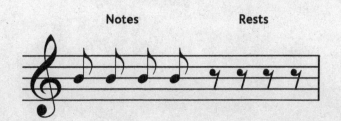

Sixteenth Note/ Semiquaver Rest

The semiquaver rest is half the length of the quaver rest. It has the same length as a sixteenth note, or semiquaver.

The standard musical bar contains four beats.

A semiquaver rest lasts for a **sixteenth** of a **bar** and so has a quarter of a beat.

Notes   Rests

Quick How to Read Music

Simple Search

6

STEP 6

TIME SIGNATURES

A time signature tells us how many notes
and rests will appear in each bar of music.

The time signature determines the pulse of
the music, whether it will feel fast or slow.

Time signatures create the framework
around which the notes can be written and
understood. They organize the sound to help
the listener understand what is happening
inside the music.

Two Half
Notes Per Bar

The time signature shown with this symbol is two half notes/

minims for each bar.

The **top number** shows that there are **two beats** in every **bar**.

The **bottom** number shows the **length** of each **beat**, in this case **half**

notes/minims.

Online access
flametreemusic.com

Scan the code to
hear chords & scales

108

2
2

Two Half Notes Per Bar

The time signature shown with this symbol is an alternative to the symbol on page 109.

The C (which is short for **Cut Time**) means **two half notes/minims** for each **bar**.

There are **two beats** in every **bar**, with each of the two beats being **half notes/minims**.

Online access
flametreemusic.com Scan the code to
hear chords & scales

110

Two Quarter Notes Per Bar

The time signature shown with this symbol is two quarter notes/crotchets for each bar.

The **top number** shows that there are **two beats** in every **bar**.

The **bottom** number shows the **length** of each **beat**, in this case **quarter notes/crotchets.**

Three Quarter Notes Per Bar

The time signature shown with this symbol is three quarter notes/crotchets for each bar.

The **top number** shows that there are **three beats** in every **bar**.

The **bottom** number shows the **length** of each **beat**, in this case **quarter notes/crotchets**.

3
4

Four Quarter Notes Per Bar

The time signature shown with this symbol is four quarter notes/crotchets for each bar.

The **top number** shows that there are **four beats** in every **bar**.

The **bottom** number shows the **length** of each **beat**, in this case **quarter notes/crotchets**.

Online access
flametreemusic.com

Scan the code to
hear chords & scales

Four Quarter Notes Per Bar

The time signature shown with this symbol is an alternative to the symbol on the previous page.

The C (which is short for **Common Time**) means **four quarter notes/crotchets** for each **bar**.

There are **four beats** in every **bar**, with each of the four beats being quarter notes/crotchets.

Online access
flametreemusic.com Scan the code to
hear chords & scales

118

Five Quarter Notes Per Bar

The time signature shown with this symbol is five quarter notes/crotchets for each bar.

The **top number** shows that there are **five beats** in every **bar**.

The **bottom** number shows the **length** of each **beat**, in this case, **quarter notes/crotchets**.

5
4

Six Eighth
Notes Per Bar

The time signature shown with this symbol is six eighth notes/quavers for each bar.

The **top number** shows that there are **six beats** in every **bar**.

The **bottom** number shows the **length** of each **beat**, in this case, **eighth notes/quavers**.

In this time signature the six notes are grouped in threes.

6
8

Quick How to Read Music

Simple Search

7

STEP 7

SHARPS, FLATS & NATURALS

The notes we've covered so far in this book have been natural notes. They are played on the white notes of a piano and have the following names:

A B C D E F G

However, there are notes that sit between some of these whole notes. They are played on the black keys. These notes are half a tone (a semitone) below or above the white notes and are indicated by a flat, sharp or sometimes a natural sign.

Natural & Sharp Notes on the Keyboard

You can see here how the 12 notes work before they are repeated. For clarity at this stage the diagrams opposite just use sharp signs, although later we will look at flat signs too.

On the piano the **natural notes** appear on the **white** keys, with the **sharp** notes on the **black** keys. The difference in pitch between these and any number of notes is called an **interval**.

You can see that black notes do not appear between E and F or B and C. This begins to show us how a **scale**, which depends on different intervals, might work. We look at this later from page 179.

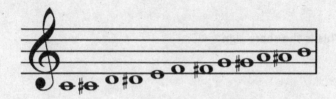

C C# D D# E F F# G G# A A# B

**Natural notes on the white keys,
sharp notes on the black keys**

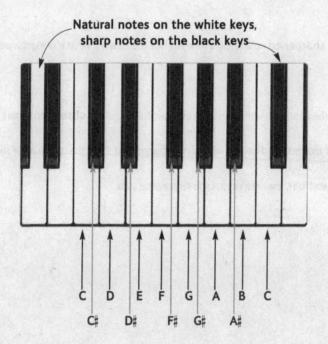

C D E F G A B C

C# D# F# G# A#

Sharps

This is the sharp sign.

It is written to the **left** of a notehead.

A **sharpened** note is half a tone **higher** than the note that is being sharpened.

When a sharp is written in front of a particular note all **subsequent uses**

of that note **in the bar** will also be **sharpened**. From the beginning of the

next bar, the note **reverts** to its previous state.

Sharp Notes on the Keyboard

Sharp notes appear on the black keys on the piano. Black keys do not appear between every pair of white keys: there is no black key between B and C, or between E and F.

So B♯ is the **same note** as C.

And E♯ is the **same note** as F.

E♯　=　F　　　B♯　=　C

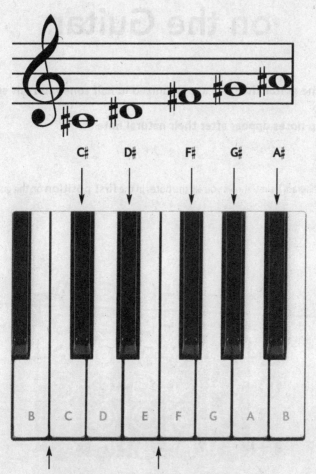

Semitone interval between these notes.

Sharp Notes
on the Guitar

On the guitar the frets are organized in half tone intervals so

sharp notes appear after their natural note.

The diagram below shows you all the notes in the **first position** on the guitar.

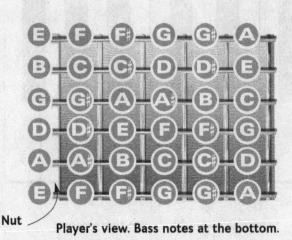

Nut

Player's view. Bass notes at the bottom.

Online access
flametreemusic.com

Scan the code to
hear chords & scales

C♯   D♯   F♯   G♯   A♯

These are the sharp notes in the octave above middle C.

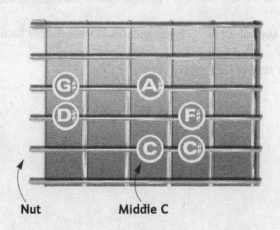

Nut   Middle C

Online access
flametreemusic.com

Scan the code to
hear chords & scales

133

Flats

This is the flat sign.

It is written to the **left** of a notehead.

A **flattened** note is half a tone **lower** than the note that is being flattened.

When a flat is written in front of a particular note all **subsequent uses** of that note **in the bar** will also be **flattened**. From the beginning of the **next bar**, the note **reverts** to its previous state.

Online access
flametreemusic.com **Scan the code to**
hear chords & scales

134

Flat Notes on the Keyboard

Flat notes appear on the black keys on the piano. As you have seen

previously, **black** keys do **not** appear between **every** pair of **white** keys: there

is **no black key** between **B** and **C**, or **E** and **F**.

So **C♭** is the **same note** as **B**

And **F♭** is the **same note** as **E**.

F♭ = E   C♭ = B

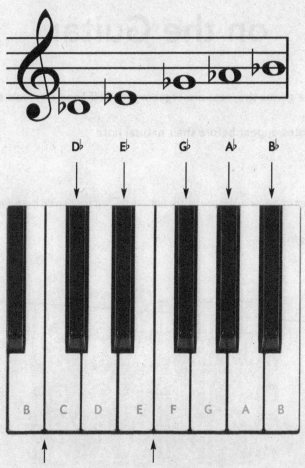

Half note interval between these notes.

Flat Notes on the Guitar

On the guitar the frets are organized in half tone intervals so flat notes appear before their natural note.

The diagram below shows you all the notes in the first position on the guitar, using open strings.

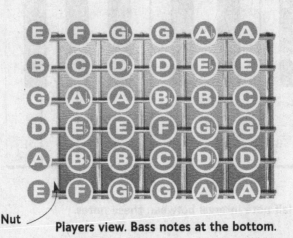

Nut

Players view. Bass notes at the bottom.

D♭   E♭   G♭   A♭   B♭

These are the flat notes in the octave above middle C.

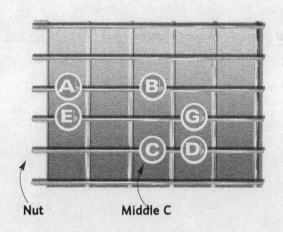

Nut   Middle C

Natural

This is the natural sign.

It is written to the **left** of a notehead.

A natural sign is used to **cancel** the effect of a **sharp** or a **flat** note played

previously in the same bar, or present in the key signature (*see* page 147).

Natural notes are played on the **white** keys of a piano.

Natural Notes on the Keyboard

Notes with a natural symbol occur when a particular note has been sharpened or flattened previously in the bar or in the key signature. Once applied, the **natural** symbol for the particular note applies for the rest of the bar unless another sharp or flat appears.

A **D♯** is a **semitone** higher than **D♮**.

A **D♭** is a **semitone** lower than **D♮**.

D♯   D   D♭   D

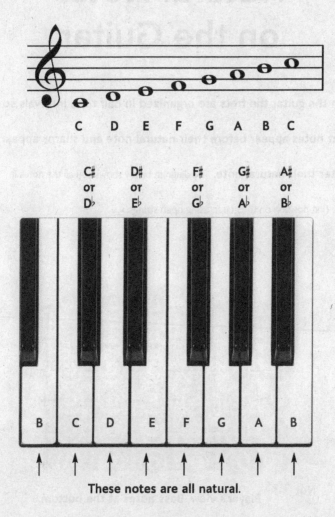

These notes are all natural.

Natural Notes on the Guitar

On the guitar the frets are organized in half tone intervals so flat notes appear before their natural note and sharps appear after their natural note. The diagram below shows you all the notes in the first position on the guitar, using open strings.

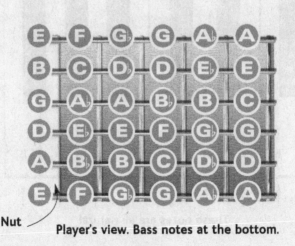

Nut

Player's view. Bass notes at the bottom.

Online access
flametreemusic.com

Scan the code to
hear chords & scales

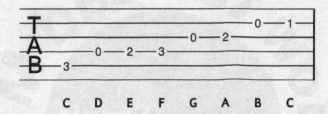

| | C | D | E | F | G | A | B | C |

Some guitarists use tablature (called TAB) instead of staff notation. Notes in TAB are shown on six lines representing the six strings of the guitar.

The low E string is at the bottom and the notes are given the fret number on the appropriate string. The natural notes are shown in TAB above and a guitar diagram below.

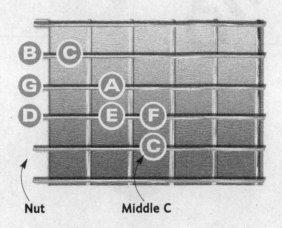

Nut   Middle C

Online access
flametreemusic.com   Scan the code to
                        hear chords & scales

145

Quick **How to Read Music**

Simple
Search

8

STEP 8

KEY SIGNATURES

The Natural notes above and below middle C are the white keys on a piano. Key signatures allow us to use the black notes, which are the sharps and flats.

A sharp or flat in the key signature indicates that these should be played each time the note appears. Each key signature contains a different number of sharps or flats (never both) and makes the music sound distinctive.

A key signature is shown at the start of each stave and is indicated by sharp or flat symbols on note lines or spaces.

Online access
flametreemusic.com

Scan the code to
hear chords & scales

Key Signature

No Sharp or Flat

C Major

A Minor

The keys of C major and its relative, A minor,

have no sharps or flats.

Key Signature

1 Sharp

G Major

E Minor

The keys of G major and its relative, E minor,

have one sharp:

Key Signature

2 Sharps

D Major

B Minor

The keys of D major and its relative,

B minor, have two sharps:

F♯ C♯

Key Signature

3 Sharps

A Major

F# Minor

The keys of A major and its relative,

F# minor, have three sharps:

F# C# G#

Key Signature

4 Sharps

E Major

C♯ Minor

The keys of E major and its relative,

C♯ minor, have four sharps:

F♯ C♯ G♯ D♯

Online access
flametreemusic.com **Scan the code to
hear chords & scales**

157

Key Signature

5 Sharps

B Major

G♯ Minor

The keys of B major and its relative,

G♯ minor, have five sharps:

F♯ C♯ G♯ D♯ A♯

Key Signature

6 Sharps

F♯ Major

D♯ Minor

The keys of F♯ major and its relative,

D♯ minor, have six sharps:

F♯ C♯ G♯ D♯ A♯ E♯

Key Signature

7 Sharps

C♯ Major

A♯ Minor

The keys of C♯ major and its relative,

A♯ minor, have seven sharps:

F♯ C♯ G♯ D♯ A♯ E♯ B♯

Key Signature

1 Flat

F Major

D Minor

The keys of F major and its relative,

D minor, have one flat.

B♭

Key Signature

2 Flats

B♭ Major

G Minor

The keys of B♭ major and its relative,

G minor, have two flats.

B♭ E♭

Key Signature

3 Flats

E♭ Major

C Minor

The keys of E♭ major and its relative,

C minor, have three flats:

B♭ E♭ A♭

Online access
flametreemusic.com

Scan the code to
hear chords & scales

Key Signature

4 Flats

A♭ Major

F Minor

The keys of A♭ major and its relative,

F minor, have four flats:

B♭ E♭ A♭ D♭

Online access
flametreemusic.com

Scan the code to
hear chords & scales

Key Signature

5 Flats

D♭ Major

B♭ Minor

The keys of D♭ major and its relative,

B♭ minor, have five flats:

B♭ E♭ A♭ D♭ G♭

Key Signature

6 Flats

G♭ Major

E♭ Minor

The keys of G♭ major and its relative,

E♭ minor, have six flats:

B♭ E♭ A♭ D♭ G♭ C♭

Key Signature

7 Flats

C♭ Major

A♭ Minor

The keys of C♭ major and its relative,

A♭ minor, have seven flats:

B♭ E♭ A♭ D♭ G♭ C♭ F♭

Quick How to Read Music

Simple Search

9

LEARN TO PLAY CHORDS SCALES
FLAMETREEMUSIC.COM
ONLINE LINKS

Online access
flametreemusic.com

Scan the code to
hear chords & scales

STEP 9

SCALES

Scales are rising and falling notes organized according to a particular pattern. All key signatures have major and harmonic minor scales associated with them, but there are other scales that allow further expression and are suitable for different types of music.

In this section we look at four scales per note: major, natural minor, harmonic minor, melodic minor. They each have a distinctive pattern which makes them suitable for a range of musical styles.

Chromatic Scale

The simplest scale is the chromatic scale because it contains

every note from the start to the end of an octave.

Every step of the scale is a **half tone**, or semitone.

Using middle C as the starting point, the C chromatic scale on the keyboard uses

every white and every **black key** from C to the next C above.

The chromatic scale for every key works in the same way, taking in all the

white and black keys, from the starting note of the key to the octave above.

Online access
flametreemusic.com Scan the code to
hear chords & scales

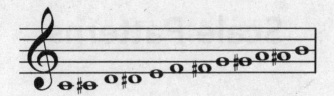

C C♯ D D♯ E F F♯ G G♯ A A♯ B

Piano: right hand fingering C chromatic scale.

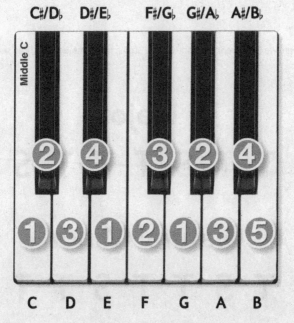

1 thumb 2 index finger 3 middle finger 4 ring finger 5 little finger

Scale Patterns

This section shows four scales for each note. Each scale conforms to a standard pattern, from the root note of the scale.

S = semitone (half step); T = tone (whole step); m3 = minor 3rd (three semitones)

Major

T T S T T T S

Natural Minor

T S T T S T T

Online access
flametreemusic.com

Scan the code to
hear chords & scales

Harmonic Minor

T S T T S m3 S

Melodic Minor

T S T T T T S

(ascending form only)

Major Pentatonic

T T m3 T m3

Minor Pentatonic

m3 T T m3 T

Online access
flametreemusic.com

Scan the code to
hear chords & scales

C Major

Scale Notes   **UP**   C D E F G A B C
DOWN   C B A G F E D C

C Natural Minor

Scale Notes

UP   C D E♭ F G A♭ B♭ C

DOWN   C B♭ A♭ G F E♭ D C

C Harmonic Minor

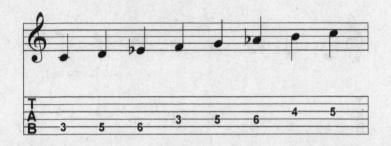

Scale Notes

UP   C D E♭ F G A♭ B C

DOWN C B A♭ G F E♭ D C

Online access
flametreemusic.com

Scan the code to
hear chords & scales

C Melodic Minor

Scale Notes

UP C D E♭ F G A B C

DOWN C B♭ A♭ G F E♭ D C

Online access
flametreemusic.com

Scan the code to
hear chords & scales

D♭ Major

Scale Notes	UP	D♭ E♭ F G♭ A♭ B♭ C D♭
	DOWN	D♭ C B♭ A♭ G♭ F E♭ D♭

C♯ Natural Minor

Scale Notes

UP C♯ D♯ E F♯ G♯ A B C♯

DOWN C♯ B A G♯ F♯ E D♯ C♯

C# Harmonic Minor

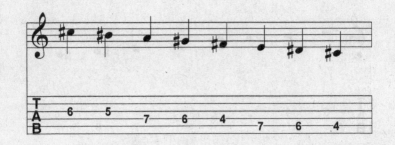

Scale Notes

UP   C# D# E F# G# A B# C#

DOWN   C# B# A G# F# E D# C#

Online access
flametreemusic.com

Scan the code to
hear chords & scales

C♯ Melodic Minor

Scale Notes

UP   C♯ D♯ E F♯ G♯ A♯ B♯ C♯
DOWN C♯ B♮ A♮ G♯ F♯ E D♯ C♯

D Major

Scale Notes

UP D E F♯ G A B C♯ D

DOWN D C♯ B A G F♯ E D

D Natural Minor

Scale Notes

UP   D E F G A B♭ C D
DOWN D C B♭ A G F E D

Online access
flametreemusic.com

Scan the code to
hear chords & scales

D Harmonic Minor

Scale Notes

UP   D E F G A B♭ C♯ D

DOWN   D C♯ B♭ A G F E D

Online access
flametreemusic.com

Scan the code to
hear chords & scales

D Melodic Minor

Scale Notes

UP D E F G A B C♯ D

DOWN D C♮ B♭ A G F E D

Online access
flametreemusic.com

Scan the code to
hear chords & scales

E♭ Major

Scale Notes

UP   B♭ F G A♭ B♭ C D E♭

DOWN   E♭ D C B♭ A♭ G F E♭

E♭ Natural Minor

Scale Notes

UP   E♭ F G♭ A♭ B♭ C♭ D♭ E♭
DOWN E♭ D♭ C♭ B♭ A♭ G♭ F E♭

E♭ Harmonic Minor

Scale Notes

UP E♭ F G♭ A♭ B♭ C♭ D E♭

DOWN E♭ D C♭ B♭ A♭ G♭ F E♭

E♭ Melodic Minor

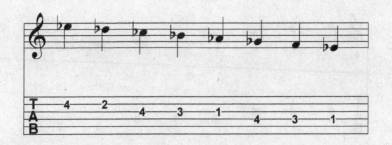

Scale Notes

UP E♭ F G♭ A♭ B♭ C D E♭

DOWN E♭ D♭ C♭ B♭ A♭ G♭ F E♭

E Major

Scale Notes

UP   E F# G# A B C# D# E
DOWN E D# C# B A G# F# E

E Natural Minor

Scale Notes UP E F# G A B C D E

DOWN E D C B A G F# E

Online access
flametreemusic.com

Scan the code to
hear chords & scales

E Harmonic Minor

Scale Notes

UP	E F♯ G A B C D♯ E
DOWN	E D♯ C B A G F♯ E

Online access
flametreemusic.com

Scan the code to
hear chords & scales

E Melodic Minor

Scale Notes

UP   E F♯ G A B C♯ D♯ E

DOWN   E D♮ C♮ B A G F♯ E

F Major

Scale Notes

UP	F G A B♭ C D E F
DOWN	F E D C B♭ A G F

F Natural Minor

| **Scale Notes** | UP | F G A♭ B♭ C D♭ E♭ F |
| | DOWN | F E♭ D♭ C B♭ A♭ G F |

F Harmonic Minor

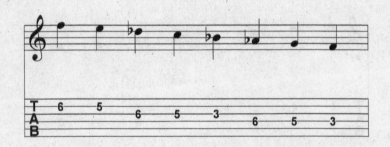

Scale Notes

UP   F G A♭ B♭ C D♭ E F

DOWN   F E D♭ C B♭ A♭ G F

F Melodic Minor

Scale Notes

UP   F G A♭ B♭ C D E F

DOWN   F E♭ D♭ C B♭ A♭ G F

Online access
flametreemusic.com

Scan the code to
hear chords & scales

F♯ Major

Scale Notes

UP   F♯ G♯ A♯ B C♯ D♯ E♯ F♯

DOWN   F♯ E♯ D♯ C♯ B A♯ G♯ F♯

F# Natural Minor

Scale Notes

UP F# G# A B C# D E F#

DOWN F# E D C# B A G# F#

F# Harmonic Minor

Scale Notes

UP   F# G# A B C# D E# F#

DOWN   F# E# D C# B A G# F#

F# Melodic Minor

Scale Notes

UP F# G# A B C# D# E# F#

DOWN F# E♮ D♮ C# B A G# F#

Online access
flametreemusic.com

Scan the code to
hear chords & scales

G Major

Scale Notes

UP G A B C D E F♯ G
DOWN G F♯ E D C B A G

Online access
flametreemusic.com

Scan the code to
hear chords & scales

G Natural Minor

Scale Notes

UP G A B♭ C D E♭ F G

DOWN G F E♭ D C B♭ A G

Online access
flametreemusic.com

Scan the code to
hear chords & scales

G Harmonic Minor

Scale Notes

UP   G A B♭ C D E♭ F♯ G

DOWN   G F♯ E♭ D C B♭ A G

G Melodic Minor

Scale Notes

UP   G A B♭ C D E F♯ G

DOWN   G F♮ E♭ D C B♭ A G

A♭ Major

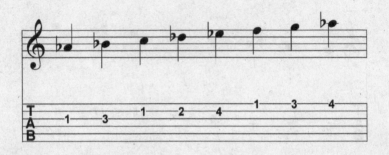

Scale Notes

UP   A♭ B♭ C D♭ E♭ F G A♭

DOWN   A♭ G F E♭ D♭ C B♭ A♭

G# Natural Minor

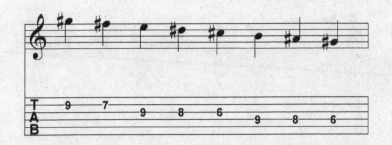

Scale Notes

UP G# A# B C# D# E F# G#

DOWN G# F# E D# C# B A# G#

Online access
flametreemusic.com

Scan the code to
hear chords & scales

G# Harmonic Minor

This double sharp symbol raises the note by two semitones.

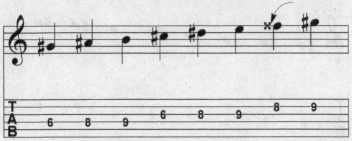

Scale Notes

UP   G# A# B C# D# E F× G#

DOWN   G# F× E D# C# B A# G#

G♯ Melodic Minor

This double sharp symbol raises the note by two semitones.

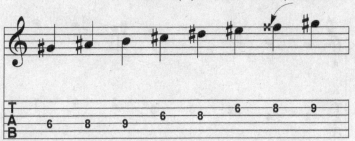

Scale Notes

UP   G♯ A♯ B C♯ D♯ E♯ F𝄪 G♯

DOWN   G♯ F♯ E♮ D♯ C♯ B A♯ G♯

A Major

Scale Notes

UP   A B C# D E F# G# A

DOWN   A G# F# E D C# B A

A Natural Minor

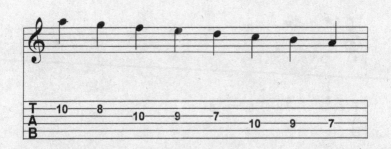

Scale Notes **UP** A B C D E F G A
 DOWN A G F E D C B A

Online access
flametreemusic.com

Scan the code to
hear chords & scales

A Harmonic Minor

Scale Notes

UP A B C D E F G# A

DOWN A G# F E D C B A

A Melodic Minor

Scale Notes

UP A B C D E F# G# A

DOWN A G♮ F♮ E D C B A

Online access
flametreemusic.com

Scan the code to
hear chords & scales

B♭ Major

Scale Notes

UP   B♭ C D E♭ F G A B♭

DOWN   B♭ A G F E♭ D C B♭

B♭ Natural Minor

Scale Notes

UP B♭ C D♭ E♭ F G♭ A♭ B♭

DOWN B♭ A♭ G♭ F E♭ D♭ C B♭

B♭ Harmonic Minor

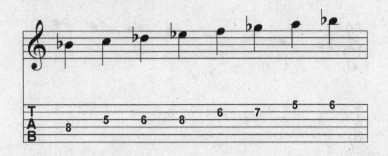

Scale Notes

UP   B♭ C D♭ E♭ F G♭ A B♭

DOWN B♭ A G♭ F E♭ D♭ C B♭

B♭ Melodic Minor

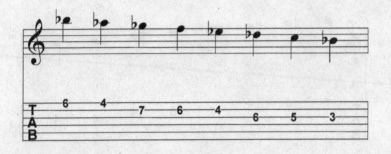

Scale Notes

UP   B♭ C D♭ E♭ F G A B♭

DOWN   B♭ A♭ G♭ F E♭ D♭ C B♭

Online access
flametreemusic.com

Scan the code to
hear chords & scales

B Major

Scale Notes

UP   B C# D# E F# G# A# B
DOWN B A# G# F# E D# C# B

B Natural Minor

Scale Notes UP   B C♯ D E F♯ G A B
DOWN   B A G F♯ E D C♯ B

B Harmonic Minor

Scale Notes

UP   B C♯ D E F♯ G A♯ B

DOWN   B A♯ G F♯ E D C♯ B

Online access
flametreemusic.com

Scan the code to
hear chords & scales

B Melodic Minor

Scale Notes

UP B C♯ D E F♯ G♯ A♯ B

DOWN B A♮ G♮ F♯ E D C♯ B

Quick How to Read Music

Simple Search

10

STEP 10

CHORDS FROM SCALES

We've looked at single notes played one at a time, so now it's time to move on to chords, which can be used to accompany single-line melodies. Chords add richness and depth to music and can be played on any instrument capable of making more than one sound at a time: such as keyboard, guitar, or harp. For rock, blues and folk musicians, chords often provide the backbone to their songwriting. Melodic instruments and voices joined together also create a chord-like sound, with many parts harmonizing in a series of chord-like structures.

How to Make a Chord from a Scale

If you know which key to start in, you can identify which chords will work in that key.

Simple chords are called **triads** because they are made up of **three notes**.

To find the simple triad chords from a scale, use **any note** within to **start**, then **add** the **note two up**, then **add** the note **two up again**.

The **root** note of a chord is the **lowest** note: for example, the C major chord will have C as its root, and D major will have D as its root.

C Major Scale

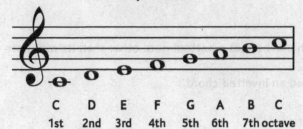

C	D	E	F	G	A	B	C
1st	2nd	3rd	4th	5th	6th	7th	octave
I	II	III	IV	V	VI	VII	

C Major chord

1st + 3rd + 5th notes of the C Major scale

G
E
C

↑
Root note

F Major chord

4th + 6th + octave notes of the C Major scale

C
A
F

↑
Root note

G Major chord

5th + 7th + high 2nd notes of the C Major scale

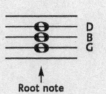

D
B
G

↑
Root note

Chord Inversions

A chord that has a bottom note other than its root note is

called an inverted chord.

Inverted chords are used to add colour and variety to a musical piece. A bass or

double bass might play the root notes while the keyboard or string players might

play an inverted chord above the root note.

As an example, the C major chord can be played with the **root note** of **C**, or the

E or the **G**.

C Major Scale

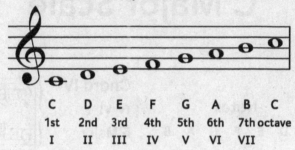

C	D	E	F	G	A	B	C
1st	2nd	3rd	4th	5th	6th	7th	octave
I	II	III	IV	V	VI	VII	

C Major chord

1st, 3rd and 5th notes of the C Major scale

G
E
C

Root note

C Major 1st Inversion

3rd and 5th and octave notes of the C Major scale

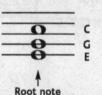

C
G
E

Root note

C Major 2nd Inversion

5th, octave and high 3rd notes of the C Major scale

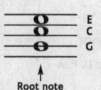

E
C
G

Root note

Common Chords of the
C Major Scale

Chord IV

IV, VI, I

F Major

Notes: F, A, C

Notes

C	D	E	F	G	A	B
I	II	III	IV	V	VI	VII

Chord I

I, III, V

C Major

Notes: C, E, G

Chord V

V, VII, II

G Major

Notes: G, B, D

Chord II

II, IV, VI

D Minor

Notes: D, F, A

Chord VI

VI, I, III

A Minor

Notes: A, C, E

Common Chords of the
D♭ Major Scale

Notes

D♭	E♭	F	G♭	A♭	B♭	C
I	II	III	IV	V	VI	VII

Chord IV

IV, VI, I

G♭ Major

Notes: G♭, B♭, D♭

Chord I

I, III, V

D♭ Major

Notes: D♭, F, A♭

Chord V

V, VII, II

A♭ Major

Notes: A♭, C, E♭

Chord II

II, IV, VI

E♭ Minor

Notes: E♭, G♭, B♭

Chord VI

VI, I, III

B♭ Minor

Notes: B♭, D♭, F

Online access
flametreemusic.com

Scan the code to
hear chords & scales

239

Common Chords of the
D Major Scale

Notes

D E F♯ G A B C♯

I II III IV V VI VII

Chord IV
IV, VI, I
G Major
Notes: G, B, D

Chord I
I, III, V
D Major
Notes: D, F♯, A

Chord V
V, VII, II
A Major
Notes: A, C♯ E

Chord II
II, IV, VI
E Minor
Notes: E, G, B

Chord VI
VI, I, III
B Minor
Notes: B, D, F♯

Online access
flametreemusic.com

Scan the code to
hear chords & scales

Common Chords of the
E♭ Major Scale

Notes

E♭	F	G	A♭	B♭	C	D
I	II	III	IV	V	VI	VII

Chord IV

IV, VI, I

A♭ Major

Notes: A♭, C, E♭

Chord I

I, III, V

E♭ Major

Notes: E♭, G, B♭

Chord V

V, VII, II

B♭ Major

Notes: B♭, D, F

Chord II

II, IV, VI

F Minor

Notes: F, A♭, C

Chord VI

VI, I, III

C Minor

Notes: C, E♭, G

Common Chords of the
E Major Scale

Notes

E	F♯	G♯	A	B	C♯	D♯
I	II	III	IV	V	VI	VII

Chord IV

IV, VI, I

A Major

Notes: A, C♯, E

Chord I

I, III, V

E Major

Notes: E, G♯, B

Chord V

V, VII, II

B Major

Notes: B, D♯, F♯

Chord II

II, IV, VI

F♯ Minor

Notes: F♯, A, C♯

Chord VI

VI, I, III

C♯ Minor

Notes: C♯, E, G♯

Online access
flametreemusic.com

Scan the code to
hear chords & scales

Common Chords of the
F Major Scale

Notes

F G A B♭ C D E
I II III IV V VI VII

Chord IV

IV, VI, I

B♭ Major

Notes: B♭, D, F

Chord I

I, III, V

F Major

Notes: F, A, C

Chord V

V, VII, II

C Major

Notes: C, E, G

Chord II

II, IV, VI

G Minor

Notes: G, B♭, D

Chord VI

VI, I, III

D Minor

Notes: D, F, A

Common Chords of the
F♯ Major Scale

Notes

F♯	G♯	A♯	B	C♯	D♯	E♯
I	II	III	IV	V	VI	VII

Chord IV

IV, VI, I

B Major

Notes: B, D♯, F♯

Chord I

I, III, V

F♯ Major

Notes: F♯, A♯, C♯

Chord V

V, VII, II

C♯ Major

Notes: C♯, E♯, G♯

Chord II

II, IV, VI

G♯ Minor

Notes: G♯, B, D♯

Chord VI

VI, I, III

D♯ Minor

Notes: D♯, F♯, A♯

Online access
flametreemusic.com

Scan the code to
hear chords & scales

Common Chords of the
G Major Scale

Notes

G	A	B	C	D	E	F#
I	II	III	IV	V	VI	VII

Chord IV

IV, VI, I

C Major

Notes: C, E, G

Chord I

I, III, V

G Major

Notes: G, B, D

Chord V

V, VII, II

D Major

Notes: D, F#, A

Chord II

II, IV, VI

A Minor

Notes: A, C, E

Chord VI

VI, I, III

E Minor

Notes: E, G, B

Common Chords of the
A♭ Major Scale

Notes

A♭	B♭	C	D♭	E♭	F	G
I	II	III	IV	V	VI	VII

Chord IV
IV, VI, I

D♭ Major

Notes: D♭, F, A♭

Chord I
I, III, V

A♭ Major

Notes: A♭, C, E♭

Chord V
V, VII, II

E♭ Major

Notes: E♭, G, B♭

Chord II
II, IV, VI

B♭ Minor

Notes: B♭, D♭, F

Chord VI
VI, I, III

F Minor

Notes: F, A♭, C

Common Chords of the
A Major Scale

Chord IV

IV, VI, I

D Major

Notes: D, F♯, A

Notes

A	B	C♯	D	E	F♯	G♯
I	II	III	IV	V	VI	VII

Chord I

I, III, V

A Major

Notes: A, C♯, E

Chord V

V, VII, II

E Major

Notes: E, G♯, B

Chord II

II, IV, VI

B Minor

Notes: B, D, F♯

Chord VI

VI, I, III

F♯ Minor

Notes: F♯, A, C♯

Common Chords of the
B♭ Major Scale

Notes

B♭	C	D	E♭	F	G	A
I	II	III	IV	V	VI	VII

Chord IV

IV, VI, I

E♭ Major

Notes: E♭, G, B♭

Chord I

I, III, V

B♭ Major

Notes: B♭, D, F

Chord V

V, VII, II

F Major

Notes: F, A, C

Chord II

II, IV, VI

C Minor

Notes: C, E♭, G

Chord VI

VI, I, III

G Minor

Notes: G, B♭, D

Online access
flametreemusic.com

Scan the code to
hear chords & scales

Common Chords of the
B Major Scale

Notes

B	C♯	D♯	E	F♯	G♯	A♯
I	II	III	IV	V	VI	VII

Chord IV

IV, VI, I

E Major

Notes: E, G♯, B

Chord I

I, III, V

B Major

Notes: B, D♯, F♯

Chord V

V, VII, II

F♯ Major

Notes: F♯, A♯, C♯

Chord II

II, IV, VI

C♯ Minor

Notes: C♯, E, G♯

Chord VI

VI, I, III

G♯ Minor

Notes: G♯, B, D♯

Quick How to Read Music

Simple Search

SYMBOLS & MARKS

A musical piece is often full of symbols, all of which provide clues about how the music should be played: how loud, what speed and when to repeat.

Classical music uses a great many Italian terms because in the early 1600s Italy was the cultural centre of European music. Church choral music moved to broader orchestral forms, the major and minor scales were standardized and tonal music gained great influence, resulting in the western classical style. The twentieth century brought an explosion of new styles of music (blues, jazz, rock) and with them the greater use of English terms.

Tempo

These marks are written above the music and show how quickly to play.

lento or *adagio*	slowly
andante	at walking speed
moderato	moderate speed
allegretto	fairly fast
allegro	fast
presto	very fast
ritardando (rit.)	slowing down
accelerando (accel.)	going faster
a tempo	at original speed
piu mosso	faster
meno mosso	slower
ad lib./ad libitum	freely

Dynamics

These marks are written underneath the notes and show how loud to play them.

pp	*pianissimo*	very quiet
p	*piano*	quiet
mp	*mezzopiano*	fairly quiet
mf	*mezzoforte*	fairly loud
f	*forte*	loud
ff	*fortissimo*	very loud
<	*crescendo* (*cresc.*)	growing louder
>	*diminuendo* (*dim.*)	growing quieter

Articulation

These marks are written above or underneath
the notes to show how to play them.

.	*staccato*	Short
>	*accento*	accented
∧	*marcato*	louder accent
—	*tenuto*	slightly stressed
⌣	*legato*	slur, smooth
sfz	*sforzando*	forced, heavy accent
fp	*fortepiano*	loud attack then quiet
⌢	*fermata*	hold, pause
8*va*	*all' ottava*	one octave higher than written
8*ab*	*ottava bassa*	One octave lower than written
tr	⋀⋀⋀⋀⋀⋀⋀⋀	trill

Other Symbols

D.C. al Fine	Return to the beginning and play to *Fine* (end).
D.S. al Fine	Return to 𝄋 and play to *Fine*.
D.C. al Coda	Return to the beginning, play to 𝄌 and skip to Coda.
D.S. al Coda	Return to 𝄋, play to 𝄌 and skip to Coda.
:‖ ‖:	Return to the beginning or nearest repeat sign.

Stems and Beams

Notes below the third line are written with their stems up. For beamed notes the note furthest from the third line determines the stem direction.

Online access
flametreemusic.com   Scan the code to
hear chords & scales

255

WITHDRAWN

LEARN TO PLAY
CHORDS
SCALES

FLAMETREEMUSIC.COM
ONLINE LINKS

SEE, LISTEN, LEARN
Make it Your Own

See our books, journals,
notebooks & calendars at
flametreepublishing.com

•

Other books in this series:
Quick How to Read Music
Quick Piano & Keyboard Chords
Quick Guitar Chords
Quick Left-Hand Guitar Chords
Quick Ukulele Chords